DATE DUE

HIGHSMITH 45-220

FIRST
BIOGRAPHIES

Wilma Mankiller

Published by Raintree Steck-Vaughn Publishers, an imprint of Steck-Vaughn Company

Planned and produced by The Creative Publishing Company
Editors: Christine Lawrie and Pam Wells

Library of Congress Cataloging-in-Publication Data

Holland, Gini.
    Wilma Mankiller / Gini Holland; illustrated by Mike White.
        p.   cm. — (First biographies)
    Summary: Describes the life of the Indian activist who became the first woman Principal Chief of the Cherokee Nation.
    ISBN 0-8172-4457-3
    1. Mankiller, Wilma Pearl, 1945- — Juvenile literature.
2. Cherokee women — Biography — Juvenile literature.   3. Cherokee women — Kings and rulers — Juvenile literature.   4. Cherokee women — Politics and government — Juvenile literature.
[1. Mankiller, Wilma Pearl, 1945- .   2. Cherokee Indians — Biography.   3. Indians of North America — Biography.   4. Women — Biography.]   I. White, Mike (Mike H.), 1939- ill.   II. Title.   III. Series.
E99.C5M3343   1997
973'.04975'0092 — dc20   96-2618
[B]   CIP
                                                               AC

Printed and bound in the United States
1 2 3 4 5 6 7 8 9 0 W 00 99 98 97 96

Note to the reader: The art on the cover shows the Trail of Tears, an important event in the history of the Cherokee people. See pages 10 and 11 in this book.

FIRST BIOGRAPHIES

Wilma Mankiller

Gini Holland
Illustrated by Mike White

RSVP
RAINTREE
STECK-VAUGHN
P U B L I S H E R S
The Steck-Vaughn Company

Wilma Mankiller walked a long path to become the first woman principal chief of the Cherokee Nation. When she was a child, her family was poor. They lived in Stilwell, Oklahoma. In Stilwell everyone was poor, so, in a way, life seemed fair. But it was hard for Wilma's parents to give their children everything they needed.

6

Even so, Wilma felt rich when she heard the stories about her people. Her Aunt Maggie told Cherokee legends filled with wisdom. Her parents explained how the Cherokees had been forced off their land long ago. It was a sad story.

Wilma's father was the son of Cherokees who wore the clothes and cowboy hats of Oklahoma. But they came from a part of the country that had nothing to do with cowboys. They had once lived in the woods and hills of the Southeast.

The Cherokees had great respect for nature and tried to live in harmony with the Earth and all living things. Wilma's mother was Dutch and Irish, but she grew up in Cherokee country. So she understood Cherokee ways and history.

The history of the Cherokee people was long and proud. But their lives changed forever when white settlers came to North America.

These settlers wanted the Cherokees' land for themselves. So in 1838, President Andrew Jackson made Cherokees give all their land, millions of acres, to white families.

Route of the Trail of Tears

Then President Jackson made the Cherokee people walk 1,200 miles through snow and killing winds to Indian Territory. This was an area of dry, windswept plains that is now northeastern Oklahoma. Of the seventeen thousand men, women, and children who started out, over four thousand died on the way. Another thousand escaped to the Great Smoky Mountains. The Cherokees still call their journey the Trail of Tears.

The Cherokees did not give up hope. In 1821, a Cherokee called Sequoyah had invented a special alphabet. This way their language could be written down. Now the Cherokees wrote laws for their new nation. They built homes, roads, and schools. Soon, more Cherokees than whites could read and write in their area of Oklahoma.

Then, in 1907, Cherokee land was taken away again. Some of the Cherokees gave up their own ways to live among white people. Others chose to live on areas of land set aside for them. These areas were called reservations.

Even so, the United States government wanted them to learn the ways of white people. They took children away from their families by force and sent them to government schools. At school the teachers lined them up and cut off their braids. The children were horrified because cutting the hair is done to show respect for someone who has died.

The teachers would not let Cherokee children speak their own language, do their traditional dances, or wear traditional clothes. Traditional means ways that began a very long time ago and have been passed down over many years.

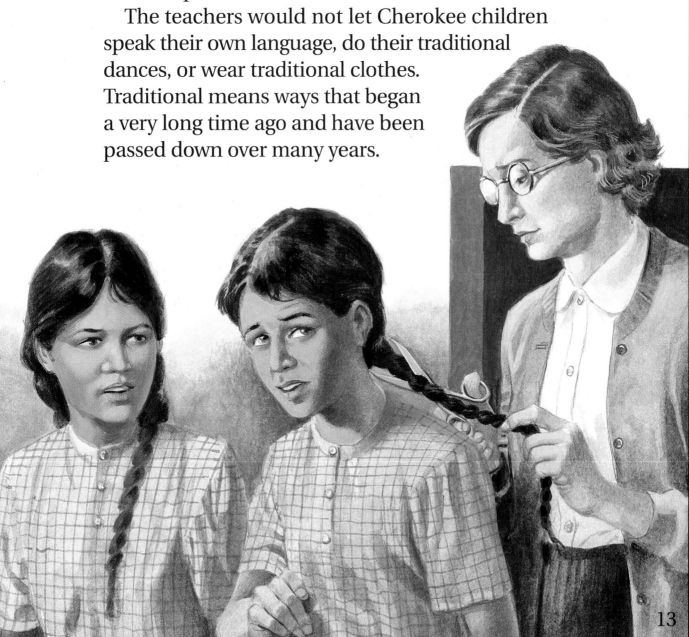

Fewer and fewer Cherokees learned to read and write. It was hard to earn a living, and the people were poor. But, by the time Wilma Mankiller was born in 1945, the United States government had begun to change its laws about Native Americans. This made it easier for the Cherokees to run their own lives again.

Wilma's family lived on their farm in Mankiller Flats. They grew their own food, but in 1956, after a long drought, the crops failed. Her father decided to move to San Francisco. The family felt as if this were their own Trail of Tears.

Wilma's new classmates did not understand Cherokee names or history. They teased her about her Oklahoma accent and her last name, which means something like "captain."

Yet Wilma was still able to go to traditional powwows with her sisters, even in San Francisco. Soon she also made friends with the African-American kids in her neighborhood. She enjoyed their friendship and their music.

After Wilma graduated from high school, she went to San Francisco State University. She married Hugo Olaya, a South American businessman, and had two daughters, Felicia and Gina. Then she started working for changes in the government and in the community.

In 1969, Wilma helped support a Native American protest on Alcatraz Island, in San Francisco Bay. The Native Americans said they were taking back tribal land that had belonged to them before white people had taken it away. The protest was an eighteen-month takeover of the island. It helped people understand what the U.S. government had done to the Native American nations so many years ago.

After the Alcatraz protest, Wilma's life changed in big ways. Earlier her father had died of kidney disease. Her mother had decided to move back home. Wilma divorced her husband. Now, she also returned to Oklahoma with her children.

Back home, she started to work for the Cherokee people. She helped them to become well educated and to find jobs. She met Charlie Soap, who was also working for the community. He could perform the traditional Cherokee dances, too. Later, he would become her second husband.

In 1979, Wilma had a scary night. For Cherokees, owls mean bad things will happen. On this night, owls were all around her house! The next day, she was in a terrible car accident. Her doctors said she might never walk again. She had seventeen operations before she was able to walk.

Then life got even worse. She got a very serious disease. She needed treatment with chemicals and more surgery. It was hard to be a mother and work for a better life for Cherokees while she was so ill. But she did it. The courage of the Cherokee people was strong in her heart.

By 1981, she was back at work. In fact, she did so well that in 1983 Principal Chief Ross Swimmer asked her to run as his deputy chief in the next election. Cherokees elect their leaders every few years. She agreed, and they won the election.

In 1985, Chief Swimmer left to become the U.S. Director of the Bureau of Indian Affairs. Wilma took over as chief — the first woman principal chief of the Cherokees.

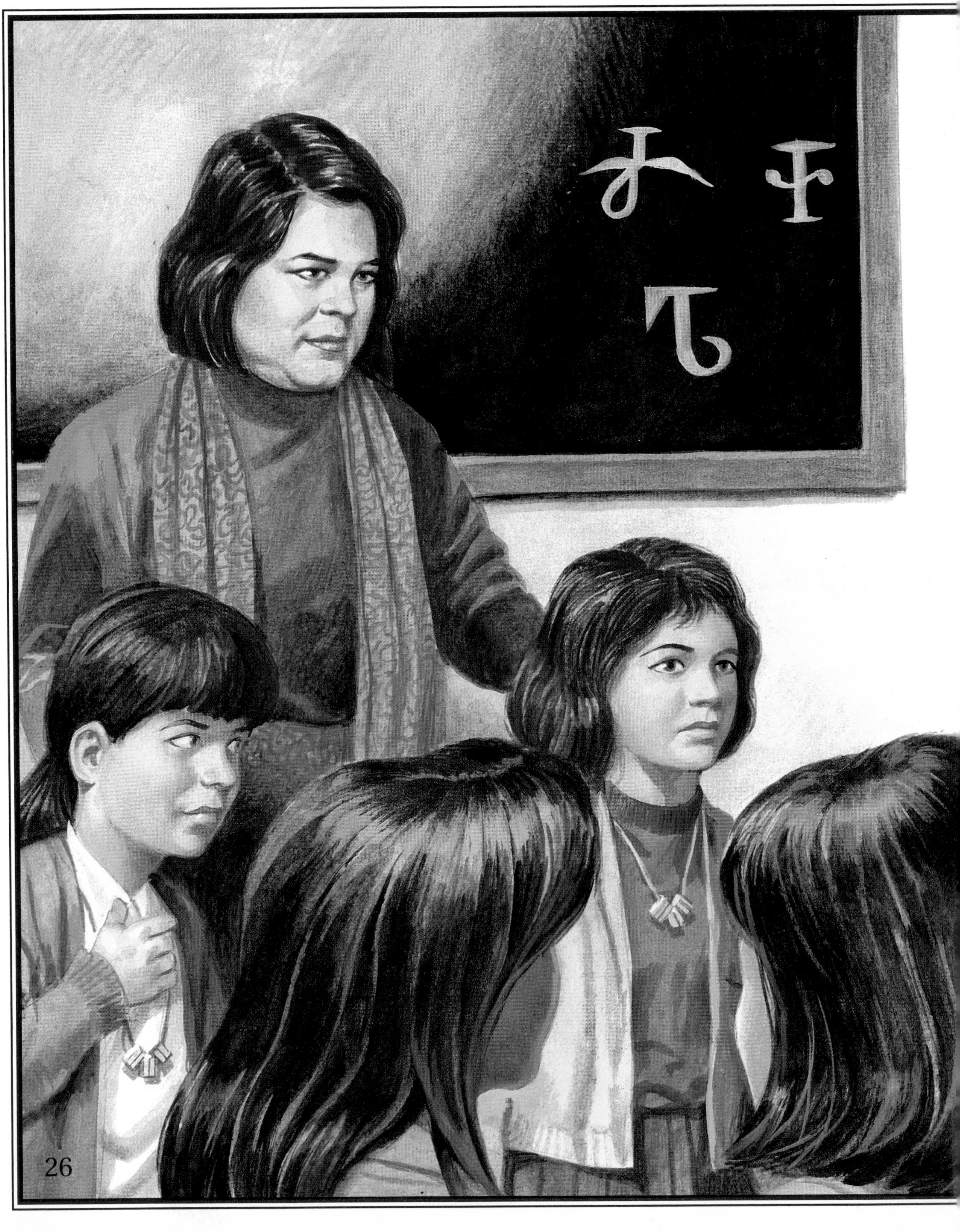

In 1987, Wilma Mankiller ran for election as principal chief of the Cherokee Nation. Before the Trail of Tears, the Cherokee clans each had a Women's Council to help decide important questions. They often decided questions of war and peace. The Cherokee people were coming back to some of the old ways of running their nation. They elected Wilma Mankiller as their chief.

Chief Mankiller wanted Cherokee children to learn about the old ways. She started a school where they could learn the Cherokee language and alphabet.

Chief Mankiller worked with her people to make the Cherokee Nation strong once again.

She governed as many people as the president of a small country. She worked with leaders from the United States and other countries. In 1988, Wilma and other leaders met President Ronald Reagan at the White House.

In 1990, Chief Mankiller signed an agreement with the U.S. government. This meant the Cherokee Nation could govern itself, as it did before the white settlers came. Now it is a nation that works with other nations. This has brought peace, health, and a good life to the Cherokee people.

In 1990, Chief Mankiller needed a kidney
transplant. Her brother Louis Donald gave her
one of his kidneys and saved her life. After that,
as chief, she worked with her people to get health
clinics, education programs, and more jobs and
businesses. She ran the Cherokee government
from 1985 to August 14, 1995. Her mother, Irene,
says "When I look at her, I just see Wilma. But
sometimes I think about what she has done . . .
and I can't believe it."

Key Dates

1945 Born in Stilwell, Oklahoma, on November 18, the sixth of eleven children.

1956 Mankiller family moves to San Francisco, California.

1969 Joins the Indian rights movement. Supports Indians who take over Alcatraz Island.

1976 Goes home to Oklahoma. Begins working with the Cherokee people.

1983 Elected deputy chief of the Cherokee Nation.

1985 Becomes first woman principal chief.

1987 Wins election as principal chief. *Ms.* magazine names her Woman of the Year.

1990 Signs an agreement with the U.S. government allowing the Cherokee Nation to govern itself. Receives a kidney from her brother.

1991 Wins election again, with 82 percent of the vote.

1992 Speaks for Native American nations at a national economic meeting in Little Rock, Arkansas.

1995 Hands over her job as principal chief but continues public speaking on social issues for Indians and women.